# In the Community

# At the Police Station

## By Julia Jaske

I see police officers
at the police station.

I see cars at the police station.

4

I see handcuffs
at the police station.

I see radios at the police station. 5

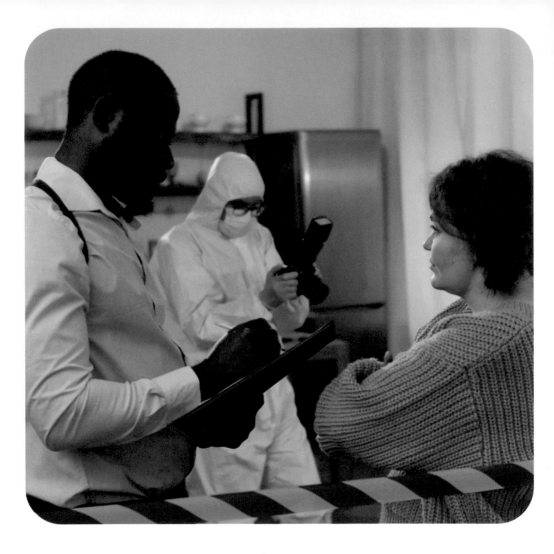

6

I see detectives
at the police station.

I see bikes at the police station

8 I see tape at the police station.

I see dogs at the police station.

10 I see badges at the police station.

I see uniforms
at the police station.

12 I see lights at the police station.

I see vests at the police station.

## Word List

police       radios       badges

station    detectives   uniforms

officers     bikes      lights

cars        tape       vests

handcuffs    dogs

- I see police officers at the police station.
- I see cars at the police station.
- I see handcuffs at the police station.
- I see radios at the police station.
- I see detectives at the police station.
- I see bikes at the police station.
- I see tape at the police station.
- I see dogs at the police station.
- I see badges at the police station.
- I see uniforms at the police station.
- I see lights at the police station.
- I see vests at the police station.

## CHERRY BLOSSOM PRESS

Published in the United States of America by Cherry Lake Publishing Group
Ann Arbor, Michigan
www.cherrylakepublishing.com

Book Designer: Keri Riley

Photo Credits: cover: © Fractal Pictures/Shutterstock; page 1: © John Roman Images/Shutterstock; page 2: © LightField Studios/Shutterstock; page 3: © antoniodiaz/Shutterstock; page 4: © Dusan Petkovic/Shutterstock; page 5: © John Roman Images/Shutterstock; page 6: © nimito/Shutterstock; page 7: © Steve Hamann/Shutterstock; page 8: © Gorodenkoff/Shutterstock; page 9: © K9 and photography/Shutterstock; page 10: © Amir Aziz/Shutterstock; page 11: © Krakenimages.com/Shutterstock; page 12: © Gorodenkoff/Shutterstock; page 13: © FeyginFoto/Shutterstock; page 14: © Fotokostic/Shutterstock

Note from publisher: Websites change regularly, and their future contents are outside of our control. Supervise children when conducting any recommended online searches for extended learning opportunities.

**Cherry Blossom Press** is an imprint of Cherry Lake Publishing Group.

Library of Congress Cataloging-in-Publication Data

Names: Jaske, Julia, author.
Title: At the police station / written by Julia Jaske.
Description: Ann Arbor, MI : Cherry Blossom Press, [2023] | Series: In the
   community | Audience: Grades K-1 | Summary: "At the Police Station
   explores the sights and sounds of the police station. It covers people
   and objects found at the police station. Uses the Whole Language
   approach to literacy, combining sight words and repetition to build
   recognition and confidence. Simple text makes reading these books easy
   and fun. Bold, colorful photographs that align directly with the text
   help readers with comprehension"— Provided by publisher.
Identifiers: LCCN 2023003172 | ISBN 9781668927212 (paperback) | ISBN
   9781668929735 (ebook) | ISBN 9781668931219 (pdf)
Subjects: LCSH: Readers (Primary) | Police stations—Juvenile literature. |
   LCGFT: Readers (Publications).
Classification: LCC PE1119.2 .J3674 2023 | DDC 428.6/2—dc23/eng/20230221
LC record available at https://lccn.loc.gov/2023003172

Printed in the United States of America
Corporate Graphics